ANIMALS!

Endangered
TUNDRA ANIMALS

Marie Allgor

PowerKiDS press.

New York

Published in 2013 by The Rosen Publishing Group, Inc.
29 East 21st Street, New York, NY 10010

First Edition

Editor: Jennifer Way
Book Design: Julio Gil

Photo Credits: Cover, pp. 6, 12, 13, 14, 15 (main, inset), 16, 17, 18 (inset), 21, 22 Shutterstock.com; pp. 4, 11 RFCD GeoAtlas; p. 5 Max Dereta/Workbook Stock/Getty Images; p. 5 (inset) © Jerry Kobalenko/Age Fotostock; p. 7 Gordon Wiltsie/National Geographic/Getty Images; p. 8 Hemera/Thinkstock; p. 9 Tom Brakefield/Stockbyte/Thinkstock; p. 10 Photos.com/Thinkstock; p. 11 Tom Ulrich/Oxford Scientific/Getty Images; pp. 18–19 © Dinodia/Age Fotostock; p. 20 Paul E. Tessier/Photodisc/Getty Images.

Library of Congress Cataloging-in-Publication Data

Allgor, Marie.
  Endangered tundra animals / by Marie Allgor. — 1st ed.
      p. cm. — (Save Earth's animals!)
  Includes index.
  ISBN 978-1-4488-7421-7 (library binding) — ISBN 978-1-4488-7494-1 (pbk.) —
ISBN 978-1-4488-7568-9 (6-pack)
  1. Endangered species—Polar regions—Juvenile literature. 2. Tundra animals—Polar regions—Juvenile literature. 3. Wildlife conservation—Polar regions—Juvenile literature. I. Title.
  QL104.A457 2013
  591.68—dc23
                            2011049573

Manufactured in China

CPSIA Compliance Information: Batch # WKTS12PK: For Further Information contact Rosen Publishing, New York, New York at 1-800-237-9932

Contents

Welcome to the Tundra!

The tundra **biome** is the coldest biome on Earth. It is a place where the ground is always frozen. It also has fewer kinds of plants and animals living in it than other biomes. Despite all this, the tundra is one of Earth's major biomes.

This map shows where tundra biomes are found.

The Tundra Biome

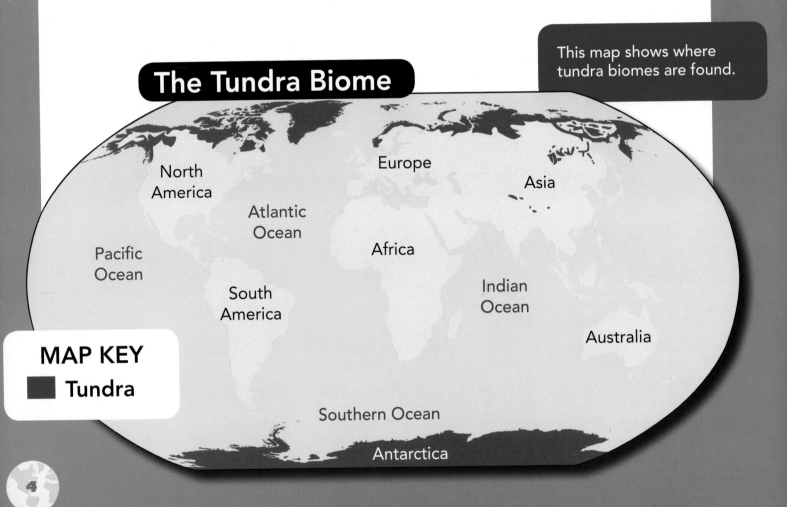

North America

Europe

Asia

Atlantic Ocean

Pacific Ocean

Africa

South America

Indian Ocean

Australia

MAP KEY
Tundra

Southern Ocean

Antarctica

This group of reindeer is grazing on the tundra in northern Russia. Reindeer that live in North America are called caribou.

Arctic hares live on the tundra in Greenland, Canada, and Alaska.

Living on the tundra is hard. The Earth's **climate** is changing. These changes are making life harder for this biome's animals. Some of the tundra's animals are **vulnerable** or endangered. This book will introduce you to some of these animals and explain what is being done to help them.

Tundra Climate

The tundra has a cold climate. It is so cold that trees cannot grow there. In fact, the name "tundra" comes from a Russian word that means "treeless plain."

The foothills of Alaska's Denali National Park are tundra.

Animals like reindeer make lichens and moss a big part of their diet. They are among the few things that grow on the tundra.

The tundra is known for low temperatures. It can be as cold as -30° F (-34° C) in winter. Even in the summer, it only gets to between 37° F and 54° F (3–12° C)! It also gets little rain and snow each year. The soil is poor and growing seasons are short. In parts of the tundra, there is a layer of soil called permafrost that is always frozen.

Habitats in the Tundra

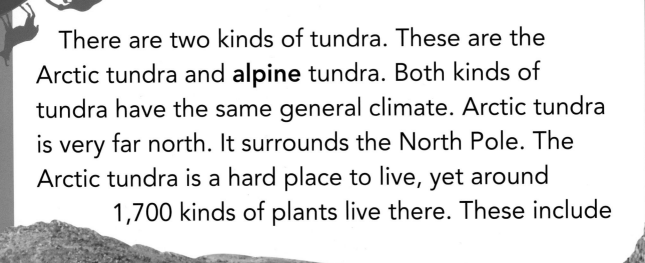

There are two kinds of tundra. These are the Arctic tundra and **alpine** tundra. Both kinds of tundra have the same general climate. Arctic tundra is very far north. It surrounds the North Pole. The Arctic tundra is a hard place to live, yet around 1,700 kinds of plants live there. These include

Bighorn sheep live in the alpine tundra.

Polar bears live in the Arctic tundra.

low bushes, mosses, and grasses. Many animals live on the Arctic tundra, too. Some of these include lemmings, caribou, arctic hares, arctic foxes, wolves, and polar bears.

Alpine tundra is high up on tall mountains. Plants that grow there include low shrubs. The animals living there include marmots, bighorn sheep, and elks.

The Tundra's Endangered Animals

The tundra is home to thousands of **species** of animals. Some of these species are doing well. Others are in trouble, though. The animals on these pages are endangered and could one day become **extinct**.

MAP KEY

- Yak
- Arctic Fox
- Siberian Crane
- Przewalski's Horse
- Siberian Marmot

Arctic Fox

1. Przewalski's Horse

This endangered horse was once listed as critically endangered. Captive Przewalski's horses have since been reintroduced into their natural habitat and their numbers are growing.

2. Yak

Wild yaks are considered a vulnerable species. This is because their numbers have dropped by about one-third over the past 30 years.

Endangered Tundra Animals

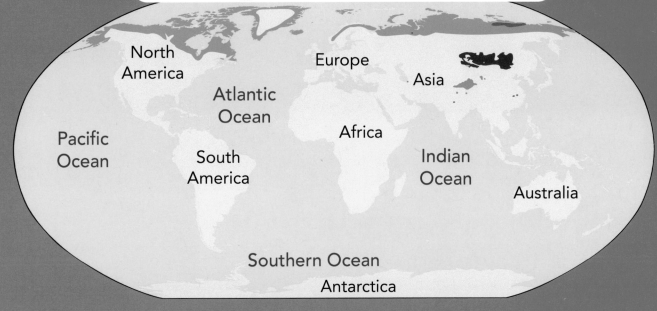

North America

Europe

Asia

Atlantic Ocean

Africa

Pacific Ocean

South America

Indian Ocean

Australia

Southern Ocean

Antarctica

3. Arctic Fox

The arctic fox is not endangered worldwide, but two of its populations are endangered. One is in Russia and the other is in Norway, Finland, Sweden, and the Kola Peninsula.

Siberian Crane

4. Siberian Crane

There are fewer than 3,000 Siberian cranes left in the wild, and their numbers are falling fast. These birds are listed as **critically** endangered. This means they could soon become extinct.

5. Siberian Marmot

The Siberian marmot is endangered mainly due to hunting. Though they are protected, these marmots are still killed for their fur.

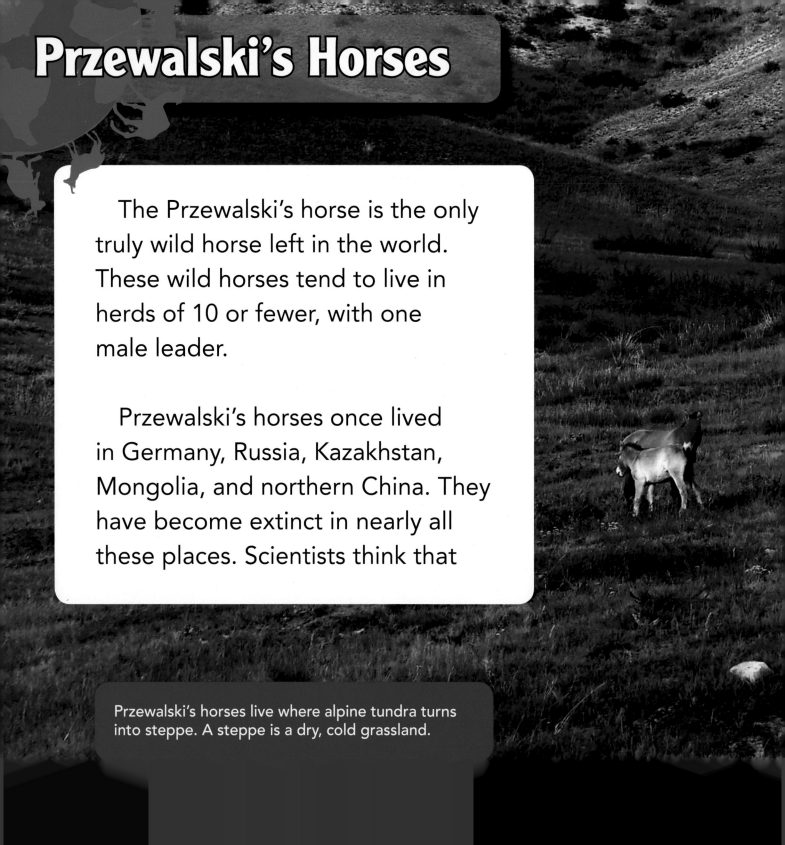

Przewalski's Horses

The Przewalski's horse is the only truly wild horse left in the world. These wild horses tend to live in herds of 10 or fewer, with one male leader.

Przewalski's horses once lived in Germany, Russia, Kazakhstan, Mongolia, and northern China. They have become extinct in nearly all these places. Scientists think that

Przewalski's horses live where alpine tundra turns into steppe. A steppe is a dry, cold grassland.

Przewalski's horses look a little different from domestic horses. For example, they have shorter legs and manes that stand straight up.

some of the reasons for this include climate change and loss of habitat as people and livestock took over land where the horses lived.

Through captive **breeding** programs, the horse has been reintroduced into the wild in Mongolia. There are around 300 Przewalski's horses in the wild today.

Yaks

Yaks are shaggy animals that are related to cows. Most yaks in the world are **domesticated**. Wild yaks live in northern India and on the Tibetan Plateau. They used to live in Nepal and Bhutan but are now extinct in those places.

Yaks graze on grasses, mosses, and lichens that grow on the tundra and in mountain meadows.

This is a domestic yak. In some places, the wild yak is losing its habitat to livestock such as domestic yaks.

Wild yaks are sometimes killed for their meat and skins. Wild yak numbers have fallen by around one-third in the last 30 years.

One of the threats to wild yaks is habitat loss caused by the spread of farms with herds of livestock. Another threat to wild yaks is poaching. Wild yaks are now protected by laws in China and in India. It is hoped that better enforcement of these laws will keep the vulnerable wild yak safe from becoming endangered or extinct.

Arctic Foxes

Arctic foxes have coats that help them blend in with their surroundings. Their coats are brown or gray in the summer and turn white in the winter. This lets them sneak up on their **prey** at any time of year. Arctic foxes are well **adapted** to life in the Arctic. Their thick fur helps them live in temperatures as cold as -58° F (-50° C)!

Here is an arctic fox with its white winter coat. These animals have fur on the bottoms of their feet to keep their feet warm and to help them walk in the snow.

In the summer, the arctic fox sheds its white coat and grows a grayish-brown summer coat.

The populations of Arctic foxes living on Russia's Medny Island and in far northern Scandinavia are endangered. Hunting and diseases caught from domestic animals are the main reasons these populations of Arctic foxes are in trouble.

These birds are critically endangered. They live in wetlands in the lowland tundra and **taiga**. There are two groups of Siberian cranes. One group

Siberian cranes have bumpy beaks that help them pull roots, tubers, and sprouts of plants out of the ground.

nests in northeastern Siberia and **migrates** to the Yangtze River, in China, in the winter. The other group nests near the Ob River, just east of the Ural Mountains, in Russia. It migrates to the south coast of the Caspian Sea in Iran each winter.

Some of the causes for the falling numbers of Siberian cranes include agricultural development, wetland drainage, oil exploration, and hunting in their resting spots. All of these things have caused problems for Siberian cranes.

The western population of Siberian cranes, like the ones here, are at risk mainly due to hunting.

Siberian Marmots

The Siberian marmot lives in the alpine tundra of Russia, Mongolia, and China. Over the last hundred years, hundreds of millions of marmots have been killed for their fur. In fact, in Mongolia, hunting led to about a 70 percent drop in their numbers in one decade! The Siberian marmot is uncommon in all the places it lives, and its numbers are going down.

The snowy owl is a bird of prey that hunts marmots, including the Siberian marmot.

The Siberian marmot is also called the Mongolian marmot and the Tarbagan marmot.

Siberian marmots live in large groups. They feed on grasses, herbs, and woody plants. People are not their only enemies. Wolves, foxes, eagles, and hawks are all marmot **predators**.

Save the Tundra's Animals!

The biggest danger to tundra animals comes from people. People hunt the animals that live there. People look for oil and natural gas in these places, too. This hurts the habitat and pollutes the environment.

The wolverine lives throughout the world's tundra and taiga habitats. It is not yet endangered, but its numbers have fallen due to habitat loss.

Luckily, many people are trying to stop hurting special places like the tundra. Laws to protect habitats help keep animals safe. This way we can share our planet with them for a long time to come.

Glossary

ADAPTED (uh-DAPT-ed) Changed to fit new conditions.

ALPINE (AL-pyn) Having to do with hills or mountains.

BIOME (BY-ohmz) Kinds of places with certain weather patterns and kinds of plants.

BREEDING (BREED-ing) Bringing a male and a female animal together so they will have babies.

CLIMATE (KLY-mut) The kind of weather a certain place has.

CRITICALLY (KRIH-tih-kuh-lee) Being at a turning point.

DOMESTICATED (duh-MES-tih-kayt-ed) Raised to live with people.

EXTINCT (ik-STINGKT) No longer existing.

MIGRATES (MY-grayts) Moves from one place to another.

PREDATORS (PREH-duh-terz) Animals that kill other animals for food.

PREY (PRAY) An animal that is hunted by another animal for food.

SPECIES (SPEE-sheez) One kind of living thing. All people are one species.

TAIGA (TY-guh) A forest with fir and spruce trees, or trees that have cones and needlelike leaves, which starts where a tundra, or icy land, ends.

VULNERABLE (VUL-neh-ruh-bel) Open to being hurt or becoming extinct.

Index

Websites

Due to the changing nature of Internet links, PowerKids Press has developed an online list of websites related to the subject of this book. This site is updated regularly. Please use this link to access the list: www.powerkidslinks.com/sea/tundra/